THE

T

CARTOONS

To Yasmin, Pat, Muriel
and all my funny friends.

THE RIGHT WAY
TO DRAW

CARTOONS

by

Mark Linley

PAPERFRONTS

Typeset in 10pt Times Roman by One & A Half Graphics, Redhill, Surrey.

Printed and bound in Great Britain by Cox and Wyman Ltd, Reading, Berks.

The *Paperfronts* series and the *Right Way* series are both published by Elliot Right Way Books, Brighton Road, Lower Kingswood, Tadworth, Surrey, KT20 6TD, U.K.

CONTENTS

1

CARTOONS ARE FUN

Now that you have joined forces with me to learn the craft of cartoonists you will have fun. I assure you that the pleasant experience will make absorbing the information an effortless process.

I will show you how to learn from the natural cartoonists: infants who are just five to seven years old. You will be taught how to turn your absent-minded doodles into funny cartoons and how to convert your own, and other folks' little weaknesses and disasters into a smile, or better still, a hearty belly laugh.

Cartoons are a wonderful way of making a point, letting off steam, or raising a giggle. Once, when I worked in an office with a nasty, incompetent bully as my manager, I got rid of my frustration by drawing a particularly horrible looking cartoon character of my tormentor. It was very sneaky of me but what a relief it gave. My chums and I had a good laugh then soldiered on. Watch out when there is an angry cartoonist about!

Imagine what fun it would be to lurk in your library, local shop or inn and jot down harmless but funny cartoons of unsuspecting customers. You could also indulge your genius while sitting in a bus, train or plane. Figure 1 (overleaf) was prompted by this remark. Notice the bold lines and lack of detail. People are the raw material of most cartoons. There is no shortage of them!

Fig. 1   Lurk in your library.

I shall first show you how to master basic cartoon drawing then move on to how to record your unique life by cartoons. "What life"? Or so you may think if your part on the world stage doesn't seem to amount to much more than work, watching television, doing household chores and sleeping. Don't worry, the most humdrum day can be changed into a delightful experience by funny drawings.

There are advantages to being a cartoonist. Your observation improves, your sense of humour expands, you may become sought after for your skill, and you could even make money with your talent. Can you picture yourself on the Costa Plonka cartooning happy tourists in return for enough loot to set you up on a palm-fringed beach for the winter? No? Think again. All things are possible! You are going to learn to pioneer in a medium which allows more freedom of expression than most other branches of art. Are you raring to go? Good. Now we shall begin.

You are special

If you think of yourself as an average sort of person who has little ability or skill you would be quite wrong. You are a Very Important Person. This notion popped figure 2 into my mind. You will find that ideas beget ideas. The more you have the more tumble through your head, sometimes so many that you need to keep a note book handy to jot them down. You will soon develop a cartoon idea brain. It happens without trying.

Look at figure 2. See how a character's thoughts are depicted in a thought bubble. This very useful device is just one of the tricks of our trade. You have unlimited possibilities for

Fig. 2   How to use a thought balloon.

Fig. 3   We all have unlimited possibilities.

achievements of all kinds. This last sentence instantly gave another idea for the cartoon featured in figure 3.

There is help in your head

You have a superb computer in your head (your sub-conscious mind) which is patiently waiting for you to programme it the right way so that you can achieve easily and quickly whatever you desire. Whether you want to draw cartoons, fly a plane or write a book, your computer will help you all the way.

How does this human miracle work? It operates simply. You just think and know that YOU CAN learn to do anything other people can do. This powerful thought works like magic. It's called *positive thinking*. Can you feel your confidence rising? It's a feeling similar to painless wind!

Off we go

Before you can begin to cartoon you have to do some work learning how to do the type of drawing required. Generally, but not always, it's an advantage to be able to sketch human and other subjects accurately. If you are unable to draw right now don't worry about it. I have ways of teaching cartooning!

Cartoons are based on life. Even the most exaggerated funny drawing, properly done, is recognizable. A sense of humour is essential to the production of humour. This may seem like an obvious statement, but not everybody has one. I had a lady on one of my cartoon activity holidays who didn't have the faintest glimmer of a sense of humour. She failed in every way! You already have the gift of laughter; otherwise you wouldn't be reading this book. Hints about developing this priceless possession will be given as you progress.

When I was a freelance part-time press cartoonist it soon became apparent that the idea sold the drawing, never the other way round. After a hard day at an asylum, called the office, it was often difficult to go home and then try to think out funny ideas for the world press. The ideas tended to come when I was fresh in the morning. After that the drawing bit was always the easy part.

A newspaper cartoonist's first task is to please an editor. This is not easy! Editors are always right. At least, they think they are. They reckon to know what sort of gags their readers like. Sometimes they do and sometimes they don't. How do I know? Friends would telephone to say that my cartoon published in the daily muck-binding Echo was rubbish! I would point out that unless I submitted that kind of joke to the paper no money would be forthcoming. The cartoons which I thought were original, and had me helpless with mirth, were often rejected. It's a tough life being a press cartoonist.

You will have no such hassle in this book. I will show you how to master each stage easily. Isn't that good news?

What you will need

The art materials you will require to start your new hobby are few and not expensive. A grade 2B pencil, an eraser, and

Fig. 4   Different pens produce different lines.

a few drawing pens will do. The latter should be size 0.1, and 0.7, and it's useful to have an art type pen (rather like a fountain pen) which will take ink cartridges, or which can be dipped into black drawing ink too. When you progress you could also add a small water colour paint brush, size 2, for use with the ink.

Figure 4 shows how each of the pens produces a different line. Notice how speech is enclosed in a balloon which is slightly different from a thought bubble. Look back at figures 2 and 3.

You will need an A5 size sketch book for those moments when inspiration strikes, and a larger A4 pad. A trick of the trade which will save your cash is to use A4 typing paper. The latter is much cheaper than buying drawing pads.

What to aim for

The best cartoons, in my not so humble opinion, are those which are funny to look at. The individual *way* an artist jots down the lines which depict his or her cartoon characters is so good that this "hallmark" itself causes the reader to smile. Some cartoonists, particularly young children, have a marvellous knack of giving each character a life of its own. You could well be another. Your aim should be to create funny people, animals or objects which amuse the viewer.

Build your cartoon characters

You can build a cartoon character from scratch. Think about Snoopy, Dennis the Menace or Andy Capp. For this book I invented a character which I named Super Doodle. This figure was based on a pretty girl who I saw. She wore feminine clothes along with huge boots. I wondered if she had an aggressive nature. Was she the sort of person who had to win? By using my observation of a fellow human and my imagination the personality of a cartoon creation was born. It is not simply a matter of producing a funny drawing; you need to manufacture a fictional person with the strengths and weaknesses that person might have.

When thinking about characters you ought to include

yourself for good measure because you certainly will be doing just that further on in this book. Make a start by studying some of the hundreds of cartoons used daily in magazines, books and newspapers. Published drawings which occupy a newspaper column width are called pocket cartoons. You might be encouraged to learn that the majority used by editors are produced by talented part-time artists.

Whenever you look at a published cartoon notice how it has been put together. See how the background has been suggested by very few lines and how each character differs. We can all learn an awful lot by simply looking and remembering. Try copying quickly the styles that appeal most to you. If you start off by drawing in a quick bold manner it will give you confidence and you won't have time to worry about whether or not you are getting it right. If you do go wrong, so what? You can re-draw just as quickly and improve in the process. Your own unique way of drawing will develop as you go. This can happen quite suddenly with some people but it normally begins to emerge after a hundred or so drawings have been made. This might sound off-putting but it isn't. It is easy to draw twenty cartoons in half an hour once you know what you are about!

I like off-beat drawings although my own style is sometimes rather life-like. It would be hard to change my way of drawing people after years of churning them out. Drawing style evolves naturally without the artist consciously doing anything other than making many sketches.

Assignments
1. Study six different newspaper pocket cartoons; then copy them.
2. Look at as many published cartoons as you can and then choose the style that you like most.
3. Copy six pocket cartoons in the style that you have chosen.

Fig. 5

2

LEARN FROM INFANTS

Most small children are natural cartoonists. They are uninhibited. They draw with bold, confident lines. I wish that many of my adult students would do the same! If you could see the way some mature beginners hesitantly scratch about with a pencil or pen you would laugh — or cry! You, of course, will not be like that will you? No. Good!

I asked a friend, who is deputy head of an infant school in Northampton, if she would arrange for some of her pupils to draw the folk they knew. Some children began by sketching their teachers. What wonderful, happy cartoons they produced! Infants are much more observant than they are given credit for being. I re-drew their masterpieces as accurately as I could. These are shown in figure 6. Each teacher featured is smiling. They are joyful pictures even though one of the staff, the one that is bottom right in figure 6, appears to be rather menacing. Notice how each child has handled hair style, body, legs, arms and hands. They are funny to look at. What more could any cartoonist ask?

It is sad that we lose this ability to be uninhibited artists as we grow up. Many also lose the pleasure and confidence with which small infants set about drawing. Now, if infants of five years old can make funny drawings, so can you. You have the benefit of greater intelligence, knowledge, and access to books on how to draw cartoons. Think back to your own school days then draw some of your teachers in the style of a child cartoonist. This is harder than it might seem, but should be fun for you!

Fig. 6   Teachers as drawn by infants.

Begin by being infantile

Children were asked to draw the family they lived with. Figure 7 shows one little girl's impressions. Notice how she

Fig. 7 Parents and sisters by an infant cartoonist.

left out hands and arms but clearly defined the difference in dress between her father, mother and sisters. Shoes were drawn in a very neat way. I think that this is a delightful drawing. Copy these figures then put in eye pupils, arms and hands. Try to make your cartoons as pleasing as the original.

Fig. 8 Drawings of a square family.

Fig. 9   Father drawn by son.

The youngster who produced the characters for figure 8 used squares to depict the bodies of adults. Because children are small and tend to look up to adults they often draw big feet which are topped by small heads. All the people drawn were happy looking, even the dog. Re-draw figure 8. Draw in missing bits: feet, arms, hands and noses.

The little boy who drew his father, featured in figure 9, had

Fig. 10 Is there an angel about?

a good idea of how to sketch features and figures. He left out a finger on one hand, but we shall excuse this small mistake. Could you draw a similar simple cartoon of your father? I'm sure you can. Off you go.

I love the cartoon character created by a girl which I have used for figure 10. She drew circles and whirls to depict the dress, hair and ear rings. Shoes were treated simply. Hands and arms were replaced by wings. This is yet another happy picture. Study this remarkable drawing then have a shot at producing a similar joyful female.

A talented youngster of six made the original drawings for those used in figure 11. Everyone is happy, as usual, including

Fig. 11   A budding cartoonist of six.

the artist as seen in his self-portrait. I like the way he handled different hair styles. The family cat, Patch, is well drawn. It just needed the far legs to be drawn a bit shorter than those on the near side. Perspective is a problem for infants of all ages up to 90!

What did you learn from infant cartoonists?

You should have learned to draw boldly, confidently and with great freedom of expression. You may have discovered that basic simple lines can make a pleasing drawing. A different way of jotting down body shapes can work very well. A happy face is easily shown by a smiling mouth. You should have been made aware that each cartoonist has his or her own distinctive style of drawing, that each sees the human being in a slightly different way. Above all, you should have noticed that children draw with great joy and enthusiasm. It shows through. I hope that your happiness will shine from your cartoons.

Assignments
1. Draw child-like cartoons of two people you know.
2. Draw similar cartoons which date back to your childhood.
3. Look at a newspaper or magazine then choose two people to draw in the same way as a child would do them.

Fig. 12

3

DOODLE WHO?

Many people doodle whilst using the telephone, hanging about the office, waiting for somebody to shop or for something to happen on the home front. There are many opportunities to doodle in a normal week. You might be a doodler. I am but my scribbling is under control. Cartoons appear!

Doodle with doodles

If you doodle odd shapes, circles or squares, start to turn them into funny drawings. Figure 13 will show you how to go about this. See how the doodles on the left of the page have been changed into similar shapes but they are now cartoons. I simply made drawings which were suggested by the doodle shape. This is a mite harder than *deliberately* setting out to make all doodles into cartoons straight off. In other words YOU control your particular doodle so that it always begins as a basic shape that is easily turned into a funny drawing. Later you can draw cartoons straight off with a pen as I do. Try copying the finished cartoons in figure 13.

Figure 14 is an example off my telephone pad. It often has more drawings on it than words. You can use your telephone conversations, or intended ones, to inspire ideas. I have a giggle by quickly drawing an off-beat portrait of the person at the other end of my telephone line. The things people say to you can also be used to give birth to cartoon doodles.

Picasso used to doodle on table clothes which then became mighty valuable. Don't be tempted to start this way. Wait a month or two!

Fig. 13   Doodles changed into cartoons.

Fig. 14   A 'doodled' telephone pad.

Be simple

It would be wise to spend time on trying to keep your cartoons as simple as possible. With this in mind it pays first to draw in pencil, then erase any unnecessary lines before inking in those that are left. By doing this exercise you will soon learn how to use as few lines as possible. The highest form of cartoon art is suggesting form or shape whilst drawing very little. Don't be discouraged if your first attempts do not seem funny to you. It sometimes happens that what may not seem amusing to the creator is to the viewer. If your early work is child-like, be pleased. You are almost there. Don't worry if your efforts are so shaky that they resemble the work of a person under the influence of hard drinking. There are a number of famous artists who have cultivated such a style. As mentioned previously, you have a lot of freedom in this game!

You could try out your brain-children on family or friends. Be positive about practice. Draw cartoons on your small pad every minute that you can. This will quickly help you succeed. Another aid to progress is to force yourself as soon as you can to draw with a pen. Fear of failure sometimes causes beginners to be nervous about straight off ink drawing. Be brave, confident and bold! You can do it.

Daily doodle

Now that you have progressed from absent-minded doodling to controlled drawing you can practise daily, every spare moment you get. The more you do the better and faster you will become. Sketch all sorts of subjects as funny cartoons: people, animals, objects. More than one cartoonist has made a fortune from an ability to turn common things into cartoons. The Shoe People is one example, Paddington Bear another. For the moment, however, just concentrate on putting down enough lines to make an amusing drawing. Almost any kind of shape can be used for the faces or figures of cartoon people. Look at figure 15. Copy these then change the shapes into figures which amuse you.

The super doodle

It is now time for you to move on to the super doodle. You have learned how to convert odd doodles into cartoons, then how deliberately to draw cartoons as doodles. Now I want you to go to the next stage: fast, controlled, casual cartoons. Just before writing this piece I grabbed a small sketch pad, went outside my house, looked at people around and then jotted down my cartoon impressions of them. The results can be seen in figure 16. I timed this little exercise: I looked at each

Fig. 15 Turn these doodles into cartoons.

Fig. 16 Simple super doodles from life.

victim for about half a minute before drawing him in, say, ten to fifteen seconds. The whole process took all of ten minutes. Cartoon production can be quick fun! Note the whistling postman, the tall thin man, the dog with a plume-like tail. There were no ladies about at the time. I'm sure you will appreciate how these cartoons are not very far removed from true life drawings. Yours can be way out if you like. Copy these for practice.

I drew the faces shown in figure 16 in my own natural style. Notice the way eyes, noses and other features can be depicted. Remember that there are no rules. You have freedom to express your people just the way you want them. They can have huge heads, small bodies, gigantic feet or can be like stick people. Anything goes so long as it's funny to look at and resembles the real thing. To illustrate this last point I took the examples used in figure 16 then re-drew them. I simply exaggerated what had been drawn previously. Look at figure 17. Notice how I have made more of some things. Heads have been enlarged to emphasize the expressions of the postman and the child, for example. The dog was given a larger tail and a smug look. These sketches took a little longer due to thinking time — all of one minute per drawing! Copy these.

Try drawing from life for yourself. You can look at your subjects for two whole minutes then spend one minute drawing each. I spoil you but I'm sure you're worth it!

The human face is the hardest feature to learn how to cartoon although it is not all that difficult. If you play about with a pen and scribble noses, eyes, mouths and general head shapes you will quickly discover the type of thing that you find funny to look at. By all means copy my work, but never forget that your own hidden style could be better than mine. While we are all influenced to some degree by other artists, naturally we must all come up with our own thing. You can't force this to happen; it just evolves painlessly. Ask yourself what sort of drawings seem the most amusing to you. Which ones do you like? Why do you like them? What do you hope to produce?

When you decide what kind of cartoon most appeals to you, work on it like mad. Try to make it easy, fast and simple to draw. Think of ways to improve your creations. Try taking lines out or putting them in. Enjoy doing it. You could be pleasantly surprised by what may emerge during this practice. Many wonderful creations come about like this. In a short time you will have what you want even though it may not be at all like the idea with which you started. Most cartoonists change their

Fig. 17 Super doodles exaggerated.

style over the years. Sometimes it is intentional but often it is something that just slowly happens.

Complete the following assignments before going to the next chapter. They, too, are important exercises to put you on the right track.

Assignments
1. Fill two pages of your sketchbook with controlled doodles.
2. Draw very simple cartoons from life. Then work on these in the way I did for figure 17.
3. Look at newspapers or magazines. Choose photographs of people then convert these into cartoons.
4. For good measure copy figure 18.

Fig. 18

4

EXPRESS EXPRESSIONS

In this chapter I shall show you how to draw the correct expressions on the faces of your cartoon characters. You can sometimes tell the mood of fellow humans by the way they set their facial features. Some folk, however, hide their feelings behind a dead-pan face. Others give away their thoughts and moods. What can we see in another person's face? There are scores of moods reflected in many different permutations. Happiness, sadness, worry, shyness, cunning, anger, joy, surprise and lots of other emotions. A cartoonist simply exaggerates what is seen so that a reader instantly knows what the cartoon character feels.

Important lines

Because you are most likely to be a happy person I shall first show you how to draw happy faces. The mouth line clearly shows when someone is in a happy mood; it curves upwards. The eyebrows may stay still; more often they arch or tighten up slightly. Have a look at figure 19. Notice how a smile can be extended into great mirth or joy, as in the bottom sketches. You will see that eyes can help to determine mood. They can seem to become round, or narrow, or may even close. There can be tears of joy flying about as well! Copy the examples in this figure with a pen.

A gloomy facial expression is the opposite of a happy one. The mouth lines go *down* while the eyebrows either remain up, stay fairly straight or turn down towards the nose. Anger or

Fig. 19   Draw happy faces.

Fig. 20   How to depict unhappy faces.

fury are progressions of gloom. These are the lower
illustrations in figure 20. Copy these cartoon faces.

Fig. 21   A frontal cartoon face.

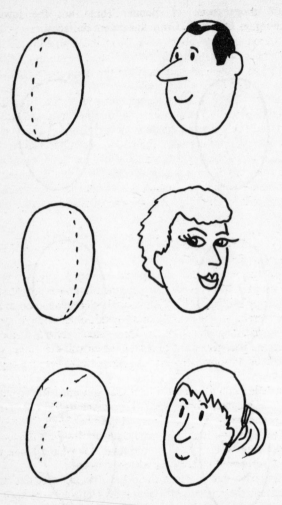

Fig. 22   Construct your cartoon faces.

Invent your own head!

Scribble down a page or two of oval shapes to use as cartoon heads. Then play about with a pencil. Begin with a frontal face. Look at figure 21 to see how this is done. You can practise by drawing frontal heads, profile ones (from the side) and then in-between ones, as in figure 22. For the latter, pencil in a dotted guideline, as shown, to help position the main features; then construct a face from that.

Figure 23 shows different cartoon faces in profile. I usually begin by drawing in big noses for my fictional men and small ones for ladies. See how I have drawn each feature. Then have a go at drawing your versions. Figure 24, of semi-frontal faces, is worth studying before you copy it. Now you have basic face shapes from which to work or develop. You can experiment with oblongs, circles, squares or whatever. Remember, however, that a cartoon must be recognizable as the real subject.

Put on your funny face

Before attempting other moods and feelings I will give you a good tip which will help you to capture different expressions. Use a mirror and yourself! It is important to relax and observe yourself carefully. You will learn an awful lot by doing a spot of acting, watching what your face does when it reflects a mood or emotion. You may want to do this when you are alone, or you might be a happy extrovert who can perform before a huge audience!

Your acting could be so brilliant that you are tempted into thoughts of a career on the stage. My advice to 9½ out of 10 of you is to dismiss any such ideas. Remember Noël Coward's song 'Don't put your daughter on the stage, Mrs Worthington!' For most of us who must go on the stage it is wise to think in terms of scrubbing it daily for a steady wage!

Friends have told me that when I'm drawing cartoons my face registers the expressions I put on my characters. Strangers who witness this amazing scene tend to think that I am quite mad!

The next part of this fun exercise is to jot down quickly the important lines you see when you are pulling faces at yourself.

Fig. 23 Faces in profile.

Fig. 24 A collection of expressions.

Start with the easy expressions, happiness and gloom, then progress to anxiety, surprise, disdain, bewilderment, and any others that you might fancy. The drawings in figure 24 cover some of the expressions mentioned. Close examination of many published cartoons will help you quickly to get the hang of this skill.

Fig. 25   "Look, Gran! An ape has escaped!"

Helpful hair

A person's hair can help to suggest what the owner is like. Untidy hair, extra long hair, neat hair and hair standing on end each give strong clues. Take another look at figures 23 and 24 and then copy those examples. Notice how filling in with ink has been used. When drawing hair styles aim to get what you want with as few lines as possible. It pays, over and over again, to simplify cartoons. Do you remember how children draw hair?

You may have noticed how cartoonists draw young ladies. Some are drawn as glamorous pin-ups with exotic heads of hair while others are sketched to raise a laugh. It's we fellows who are mostly drawn as ugly, ape-like creatures. This observation gave rise to the cartoon and caption in figure 25.

Put a lid on it

Now that you have drawn heads think about putting lids on them. Hats for men are not so popular as they once were though cartoon characters often have them. Headgear is more frequently seen on ladies. It comes in all shapes and sizes. You can invent your own if you wish. Take a glance at those drawn for figure 26. Copy them and then design a couple of your own.

Choose your eyes

You should now practise drawing eyes for your cartoon characters. Each artist seems to have a pet way of depicting eyes. It's easier to portray an attractive young lady by exaggerating her eyes as in figures 23 and 24. You will see in those examples that the size of the eyes has been increased and long eyelashes are tacked on where the character requires them. Some cartoon people have tiny dots for eyes and others have lidded peepers. You should play about with a page full of different kinds of eyes, then concentrate on the type which you like the best. Look back at some of the earlier figures for examples of different cartoon eyes.

Face types

The shape of a face can suggest the type of person it belongs to. Cartoonists tend to portray a simple person as having little forehead, with the eyes set high up. Intelligence, on the other hand, is often depicted by giving the person an egg-shaped head, with the eyes positioned low down and hidden behind

Fig. 26 Give hats to your characters.

Fig. 27 Two different face shapes.

glasses. Figure 27 illustrates these techniques. In actual fact this theory is nonsense, but it works in cartoons. There is no end to the range of face shapes that you may use for your creations. Some cartoonists have characters with square heads. You are free to do your own thing.

An average sort of face can be suggested by drawing a simple oval shape and putting in the mouth as a straight line. Making the face expressionless is an aid a cartoonist might use to show

Fig. 28 Neutral expressions.

a straight or stooge character, a listener, a silent witness or a bystander. Figure 28 will give you an idea of this type of character. Copy these examples.

Assignments
1. Draw cartoon faces of both sexes expressing the following moods: surprise, worry, anger, laughter and shock. If in doubt, use yourself and a mirror, or enlist a friend.
2. Draw two different hair styles for men and women. Draw two people wearing hats.
3. Draw a cartoon containing an angry person shouting at a worried looking character of either sex.
4. Copy the end-of-chapter super doodle saga from now on.

Fig. 29

5

FUNNY FIGURES

Drawing faces and expressions is the hardest part of this book. Now–you can start the easy bits. You need to create a cartoon body for the head that you have previously designed. Bodies, like faces, come in a wide variety of sizes and shapes and abilities to get into trouble: tall, thin, fat, short, round, angular and combinations of these. You can convert almost any odd shape into a cartoon body. Study figure 30. See how easy it is? If you start off with a basic shape which is already like a human body then the job is even easier. Some artists use the shape they have invented for all their characters. I prefer to base mine on real people; then I stretch or contract my first drawing of them as required. Experiment until you find what suits you.

Copy the examples in figure 30. Then draw in the missing heads. Try to work straight off with a pen. Move next to figure 31. These are the pre-formed bodies rather than odd shapes. See how I have drawn footwear, limbs and hands. It isn't always necessary to draw five-finger hands; you can get away with just three or four due to the wide degree of artistic licence allowed to all cartoonists. Draw all the figures and then jot in the heads. The two lower figures have their backs to you but you could make the faces so they look left or right rather than just drawing the backs of their heads.

Perhaps it is just as well that the majority of cartoons feature clothed characters. A cartoonist needs to keep an eye on current fashions, but not to the extent required of commercial

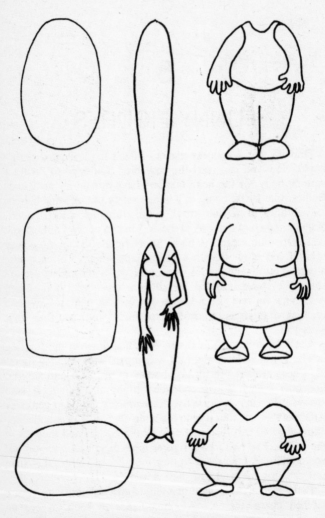

Fig. 30 How to turn odd shapes into cartoon bodies.

Fig. 31   Draw these headless bodies.

Fig. 32   Record what some people wear.

artists or designers. Some cartoonists tend to draw their men in ageless, nondescript suits or clothes (a bit like my wardrobe!). Readers spend only a split-second looking at cartoons so the clothes characters wear are not all that important. In Chapter 12 — when you may come to tell the story of your life through cartoons — you will probably have to recall past fashions. If you are a lady I expect this will be easy for you. When you churn out drawings from life you can't go wrong because nowadays everybody is dressed so differently. There is an amazing range of garments. It is not like the bad old days when the working class all dressed alike as did, for their parts, the middle and the so-called upper classes. Teenagers tend to follow their own fashions while the rest of us put on what we like.

Many people wear a uniform: policemen, traffic wardens, soldiers, etc. You might try dressing your own cartoon characters in uniforms just for practice. A very good way to do so is to record in your sketchbook what people you see are wearing at the time. Figure 32 will give you an idea of this. I used my size 2 paint brush and drawing ink to block in the black areas.

Bunches of bananas

Cartoon characters can have hands drawn with fingers looking like a bunch of bananas or sausages but they must be recognizable as hands! The best way to learn how to draw hands and fingers is to use your own as models. Those of friends, spouses or unsuspecting victims can also be used. Figures 33 and 34 show examples of cartoon hands. Female hands are usually drawn thin and long with painted finger nails. A cartoonist can get away with sketching four or even three fingers. Children usually manage to draw five fingers but sometimes they don't quite fit onto the end of the arm. Beginners tend to make fingers and hands too small. Not that this matters much in an off-beat cartoon but it does make the drawing harder. It is much easier to draw them large than it is to draw them small.

Big feet

Many cartoonists love to give their people gigantic feet. It seems to work, as do boat-like shoes. Anything seems to go. One exception appears to be that elegant ladies are usually given high-heeled shoes. Old battle-axes, poor dears, are drawn wearing clog-type monstrosities. I have drawn a small selection of shoes for figure 35. Copy these. Then invent a few designs of your own. I once asked a group of would-be

Fig. 33 Draw hands like bunches of bananas.

cartoonists to sketch each other's footwear as cartoons. They came up with some spectacular designs.

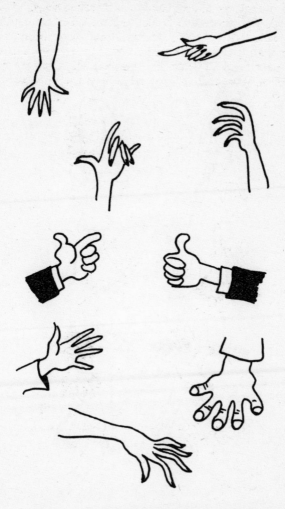

Fig. 34 See how female hands can be drawn.

Fig. 35   You can draw big feet.

Fig. 36 Stick figures can help you.

Action figures

If you are new to drawing, stick figures can help you. First, think out what the body is doing. Where should the legs and arms be? If you don't know the answer ask a friend to pose, use a mirror or look at photographs. Draw the stick figure to get the pose; then thicken it out to portray what you want. Study figure 36. It helps, by the way, to have one or more characters showing feelings as well. Their simple reactions to shock, pleasure, fear, surprise, joy and so on can be deliberately exaggerated.

Body language

Become aware of what people do. Be a person watcher. Notice how people sit, stand, walk, talk and so on. We are told that most of us give away our intentions by body language. Get into the habit of jotting down a quick sketch or even a stick figure based on what you see. This is good fun, especially if the model is unaware of what you are doing.

Assignments

1. Look at three different people then draw an outline shape for each of their bodies.
2. Convert the shapes drawn into funny figures. Don't be afraid to exaggerate your figures. Add the heads.
3. Watch a crowd of folk. Draw as many stick people as you can and then turn them into funny cartoons.

Fig. 37

6

FEATURE CREATURES

Cheep, cheep

In this chapter we shall feature creatures as funny cartoons. I have always found that birds are simple to create in a comical way. I begin by scribbling away with a pencil at the basic shape of a bird until something emerges. Figure 38 will show you how I construct a bird cartoon. Notice that the body and head start as oval forms; the beak, wings and tail are roughly triangular. A large eye is drawn in. When I am satisfied with a pencil sketch I refine it with details: the eye pupil, a suggestion of feathers, the mouth line and then the feet. Lastly I go over my drawing with a size 0.1 pen and, once it is dry, rub out the pencil marks. A new cartoon is born!

Before you tackle birds, animals or fish remember the great importance of *constructing* every drawing that you do, *starting* from the correct basic shape of the particular creature you have chosen. I can't stress too much how vital this is. A beginner cartoonist's worst mistake is to imagine, or indeed to look at, what they are drawing and then try to start on some detail such as a beak. This is the wrong way to go about the job because you are likely to get it out of proportion and, very shortly, the whole thing becomes a mess. If, however, you *build* the basic construction lines as your first step, the rest becomes very easy — just a matter of popping in the details. Apply this simple rule to all your art and you will make rapid progress. You will soon surprise yourself, your friends, and maybe even your bank manager!

Fig. 38   How to construct a bird cartoon.

Fig. 39 Draw these birds.

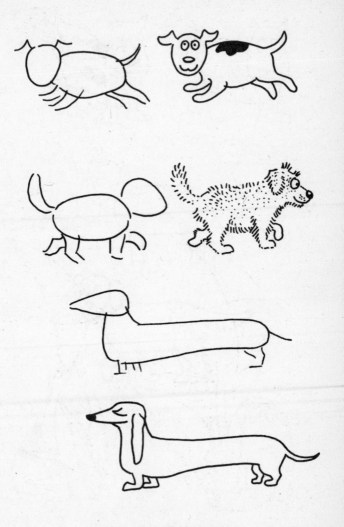

Fig. 40 Build dog cartoons.

Fig. 41 Some of the many breeds of dog.

You are now ready to copy the birds in figure 38. There are more feathered friends drawn for figure 39: a tatty looking song bird, a sad-faced duck, a bird of prey, a cross-eyed woodpecker (high-speed drilling must be hard on their beaks and bones) and a little swallow. Think out the basic shapes for the last two first; then copy the lot. You don't have to stick to what I have done. Do your own thing!

Dogs galore

"Man's best friend" was always a thought applied to dogs, but now I have my doubts. There are an awful lot of badly trained, badly handled guard dogs about. Some of these lethal animals are man's worst enemy! The average house dog, thank goodness, is usually a happy, harmless pet which lends itself to cartooning. We shall use our skill on him. Study figure 40. See how I have drawn the basic shape of each dog before refining it into a finished cartoon. Note how eyes and mouth, as in people, can denote mood. The little hairy dog was drawn with short pen strokes. Fur texture was further suggested by dots and dashes.

The many breeds of dog give us cartoonists a wide choice of subject. Figure 41 shows a few of them. The bull terrier at the top of the page was inspired after watching an old film of Oliver Twist. It stuck in my mind for some reason. The retriever (middle sketch) was given a sloppy but friendly look which reflects the temperament of these pets. (I hope no reader has been bitten by one!) I put a crown on the head of the King Charles spaniel. It was a pretty obvious thing to do but we can't all be brilliant all the time!

Comical cats

The cartoons drawn for figure 42 were not far removed from life. I simply worked on the eyes and mouth. Small changes sometimes give the best results for me. If your natural style is off-beat or wildly exaggerated stick to it; don't be influenced by my work. Beginners, by the way, often try too hard. This results in tight, over-crowded drawings with the humour blotted out by detail. The aim, once again, is to produce a

Fig. 42   Draw comical cats.

funny picture. Copy the cats in figure 42.

I invented an alley cat for figure 43. It is a bit cunning but interesting (which reminds me of a former lady friend!). Did you know that if a cat approaches you with its tail held straight up it is giving you a welcome sign? Now I know this I always stop to give a gentle pat and a few kind words. I know that you will do the same. See what you can do with the examples in figure 43.

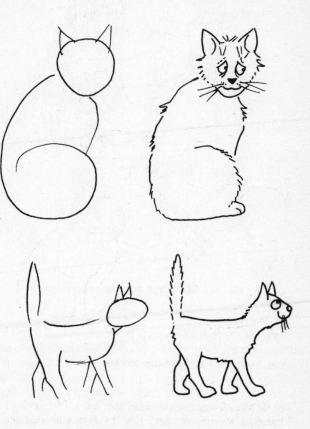

Fig. 43 Cartoon alley cats.

Fig. 44 Draw large animals as cartoons.

Draw big ones

Animals are popular subjects for greetings cards, children's books, cartoon films and many other commercial projects. I reckon almost every known creature is worthy of a funny drawing. It is possible to invent new animals. ET, of movie fame, is one good example. Large animals are perhaps slightly easier to sketch than small ones. The horse in figure 44 was deliberately drawn with shaky lines to show you what you can get away with doing. I made the legs rather like those of a pantomime horse just for fun. Pigs are quite comical to look at so making them into cartoons is relatively simple. In my example I worked on the face but left the body more or less life-like. The giraffe was treated in a similar fashion. Again, small changes work for my style.

Assignments
1. From a photograph draw a cartoon elephant.
2. Draw a cartoon of the family pet or that of a neighbour.
3. Cartoon an owl, a pigeon, or a crow.

Fig. 45

7

DRAW FUNNY THINGS

The ability to turn ordinary things into amusing cartoons is easy to learn. It need be no more than an extension of controlled doodling. The trick is to think out simple ideas and then apply them to chosen subjects.

I used a leek, an onion and an old carrot for the examples in figure 46. I turned the leek upside down to create a cartoon character; the onion was placed on its side (which suggested a comic fish to my cartoon brain); the carrot was moved around until the funny figure evolved for the bottom sketch. By using this method it should be possible to change any object into a cartoon. Try it for yourself, but don't try too hard! Just let it happen. Copy figure 46. Use your own ideas on the faces.

Cartoons can be teaching aids

Readers of my other books (see back cover) will have noticed that I use cartoons in all my writing. I have found that using them makes the text more light-hearted, and that it often provides a good way of making a point.

When I once worked on health promotion in primary schools I was required to give a session on 'Healthy Hearts'. I showed children how to draw a cartoon heart then asked them to draw their versions showing different physical activities which were good for the heart. Some of the ideas I used are shown in figure 47. Notice how simple drawing works: a big face drawn in the heart shape with small limbs and enough to suggest what sport was involved. The female hearts, of course, were pretty.

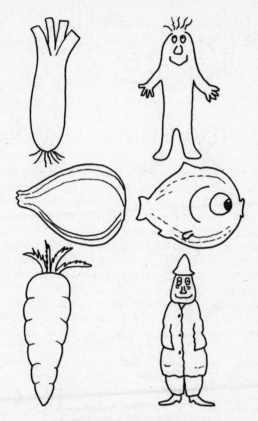

Fig. 46 Draw funny things.

On other school projects I used popular cartoons to put over information. Children always found these sessions fun. It was sometimes difficult to get them to stop in order to give me a break! The same technique was used when teaching management, communication and public relations skills to adults. Cartoons really are fun!

Fig. 47   Healthy heart cartoons.

I once had an office job that required urgent action from others in order to get my job done. Many notes and memoranda were sent out but when there was an undue delay or nothing done, I would draw a funny face or cartoon on a reminder. This almost always worked. I would receive a friendly telephone

Fig. 48 How to make books into cartoons.

call followed by prompt attention. You might have a job which could be improved by a quick cartoon. Humour is priceless.

Take things literally

I set about thinking how I could make books into cartoons. Figure 48 resulted. The two top sketches were my first thoughts. They are pretty obvious jokes: I just popped on to the book cover a face which was appropriate to the title. This idea was extended in the other drawings by having the books *do* something which used the title literally. This is a trick worth remembering, and one used by many humorists. Draw your version of figure 48.

Everything is usable

An old walking boot inspired the cartoon face in figure 49. See how I used the shape of the boot to form a funny face. The toe cap became a silly grin and the tongue a nose; eyes were then added along with a hat. With a little practice you can soon become reasonably good at this skill. You will have seen many examples of this craft used on commercial television to promote or sell various goods. There have been animated

Fig. 49   Change a boot into a face.

boxes, peas, loaves, bottles and scores of other usually inanimate objects. Now that you are a budding cartoonist you will see similar advertisements with new eyes. Knowledge of your subject can make you critical of poor work but you will learn from the good stuff.

Assignments
1. Draw a cartoon each from a pear, a tree trunk and a banana.
2. Make a cartoon based on a book on flying.
3. Look at figure 50 then think out and draw a possibility for the next exciting episode.

Fig. 50

8

HOW TO CHANGE
A HUMDRUM DAY

We may feel rather bored with life when we have a day
where nothing much seems to happen. I will show you how to
change such a day.

Create funny people

As mentioned earlier, drawing cartoons can be a fast
process. To prove this point I set myself the task of drawing
people as cartoons as they passed by. At the time a friend and
I had stopped on the interesting sea-front of Scarborough for
a cup of tea. I carried my A5 sketch pad and a 2B pencil. I used
a well-tried method of working: I looked at my victim for as
long as possible. In most cases this was a matter of seconds,
but even during this time I always took in the key points of their
overall appearance: their clothes, footwear, hair fashion, facial
characteristics and their physical build. I then jotted down a
basic figure with an exaggerated hair style and a rough face.
My total concentration went on into quickly producing a
cartoon character from what I had seen. I soon discovered that
people on the move did not re-appear for me to have a second
look at them. There was just one chance at this lark.

Figure 51 is of six quite ordinary looking holiday makers.
The girls were, in fact, quite pretty but I did not make them
so in the finished cartoons. What would they say if they knew?
The object was to make them *funny* to look at. The more

Fig. 51 Cartoon people on holiday.

beautiful a victim is, the greater the challenge to me, and, I hope, to you. Notice how I have drawn the various hair fashions, footwear and clothes. See how I have used shading to give a little depth to a line drawing. Dark colours were suggested by close diagonal lines. Try this when copying the people in this figure or doing some more of your own.

It is marvellous to see all the weird and wonderful outfits which people wear today. It is a great help to cartoonists when everybody wears something different from their fellows. The folk who were used for figure 52 are an example of this. Note the old lady clad in a thick woolly jersey and long skirt; this was surprising gear to wear on a very hot summer day. See how I drew the man who had his sweater tied round his fat neck.

It is easy to draw varied hair styles if they are depicted in a simple way. Pay attention to how I do this.

Fig. 52   A few of the wonderful outfits people wear.

Fig. 53   My passing victims.

I cartoon-captured a man here at Scarborough who I thought was typical of an elderly North Country gentleman, although he might have hailed from Brighton for all I knew! He is on the bottom right in figure 53. Note his flat cap, along with the

Fig. 54   Some folk are living cartoons.

ancient coat. A passing street cleaner I caught contemplating who knows what. The young lady, top left, had long beautiful hair (see how it looks now), shapely legs, black tights, a bulky jacket worn over a short, pleated skirt and huge boots. She was a ready made cartoon. The other lady drawn had a superb head of hair which I quickly messed up with a controlled scribble. (My own thatch is thinning so I'm jealous!) I was working at great speed, chuckling as I worked, but my mug of tea had gone cold. Did it serve me right? No, I am so glad you agree with me!

Another ready-made living cartoon character in the shape of the lady, lower right, in figure 54, appeared then disappeared before I could start to draw her. My companion and I, however, talked over what she had been wearing. Then I drew the cartoon you see. A young lady who was looking for someone was my next victim. Take note how I drew her hair and skirt blowing in the wind. My next subject was a doleful-looking dog with its owner who sported a colourful shirt. A boy running caught my eye, as did the girl walking away from where I sat. In forty minutes thirty two people were drawn. Have fun copying all the illustrations of these lovely people.

You need not go out to practise

A seaside resort offers a wide range of humanity to play about with, but what if you are stuck indoors, the rain is tipping down − with your nose trying to follow suit − and you don't have the bus fare to go anywhere? What can you do to brighten your humdrum day? "Quite a lot" is my answer! You can create your own world of imaginary cartoon characters based on any real ones you might see from your window, doorway, or on television. To test this out I forced myself to watch an old movie on TV. Take a peep at figure 55 to see what I did to two of the leading ladies and other members of the cast. There was a strident-voiced, irritating child actor in the film. I was at a loss to know what sex it was but did decide that it deserved a regular smack with a wet sock. My drawings of the actors in this classic flop improved them no end, but I won't be visiting Hollywood just yet! Isn't being a cartoonist great fun? Draw your version of the film cast.

Fig. 55   Draw the cast of a third rate movie.

Let your newspaper inspire you

A fit of madness can sometimes help a cartoonist produce funny drawings. This condition gave birth to a few wild cartoons which you can see in figure 56. At the time I had opened my daily newspaper to look at the pictures. No, not because I could not read — I simply wanted to turn some

Fig. 56 Cartoons inspired by newspapers.

people into funny cartoons. My first choice was a very famous member of our Royal family. I will not mention who it is. I might not receive a full English breakfast in the Tower of London! I next attacked, with a pencil, an up-market young lady who had been photographed at a high society bash. The state of her dress reminded me to think about buying a new second-hand shirt for Christmas. Lastly I came across a picture of a particularly handsome man. He was far too good-looking for his own good. I soon changed him! See how my normal style of drawing altered as the madness took me over. I loved every second of it. Try to become slightly mentally unhinged when you copy figure 56.

Assignments
1. Go out to any place busy with people. Then draw six of them who you see as funny cartoons.
2. Draw four cartoon characters based on some you see on your TV.
3. Choose three newspaper photographs of people; then radically change them into funny cartoons.

Fig. 57

9

LOTS AND LOTS OF STYLE

If you have copied, as suggested, all the examples and completed the assignments so far in this book you will have drawn over one hundred cartoons. A bit of your own unique style should now be beginning to show. Well done! To help you learn more about different styles of drawing cartoons, work done by ex-students of my cartoon courses has been used in this chapter.

Funny activities

During my last cartoon drawing course, participants were asked to create funny drawings about the subject of activity holidays. A gentleman, called Fred, came up with an idea which he expressed brilliantly for figure 58. This joke made me laugh. Maybe it will have a similar effect on you. Impending disaster is a theme often used by cartoonists. Notice the clean, bold lines in this example. Fred used a simple notice and a word balloon to put over the idea neatly. I know that this artist is a keen golfer. He used his hobby as an aid to obtaining a good cartoon idea. You should bear this in mind; hobbies are a wonderful source of material for you. Using your own cartoon characters re-draw figure 58.

Another project which I set my students was to take a bird, animal or reptile together with a human, and then make a cartoon of the combination. Fred had the original idea of resurrecting the extinct dodo. The result is illustrated in figure 59. You might try drawing your version of this example. I have

Fig. 58   Think of a funny activity holiday.

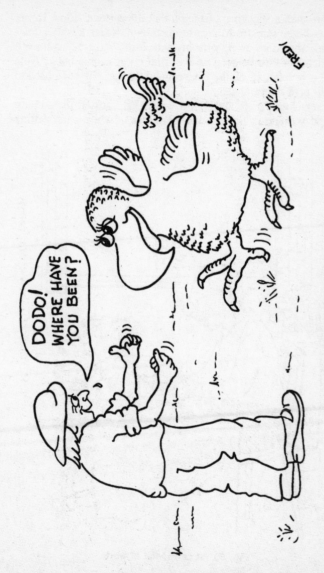

Fig. 59 A good cartoon idea.

more than a sneaking suspicion that the cartoon fellow is me. Is nobody safe from a cartoonist? No! Never mind; I have made the score even, with my sketch of Fred (see figure 60) which can also be seen on the front cover of this book. Note the way shading, on the trousers and the cat, has been used to help give depth.

My chum, mate and fellow artist, Pat, tackled the activity holiday exercise. She produced the idea of white-water rafting

Fig. 60   A cartoonist at work.

Fig. 61 White-water rafting for the over seventies.

for the over seventies! What a good idea; I wish that I had thought of it. Study figure 61. See how Pat used a size 0.1 pen to draw this sample of her cartoon style. Different sorts of shading separate individuals. Broken lines were used to suggest rough water. See how crew members are each doing their own thing.

Pat used everyday activities as the basic idea for figure 62.

Fig. 62 The author at home.

"HE GOT ALL THE WAY TO THE TOP OF SCAFELL PIKE, THEN HE CHOKED ON A BAR OF KENDAL MINT CAKE!"

Fig. 63

The cartoon victim is, again, me. Pat drew this from memory. She said it was a picture of me trying to do several things at the same time. This is true. See how Pat has used shading on the floor, desk, word processor and the cat. The figure has been drawn with a 0.5 pen to make it stand out more. Dots on the sweater suggest texture and close lines depict shadow on the trousers. Observe how all the bric-a-brac of my cluttered kitchen has been drawn. Am I really this untidy? No, of course I am not. I'm sometimes much worse!

Remember that everyday activities can be a never-ending source of ideas for you. You simply make them larger and funnier than life. Newspapers, magazines and television programmes often cover the strange activities folk get up to. Keep on the look out for off-beat happenings to use as cartoons.

A few years ago I had on my cartoon course a student named John who had great natural talent and a lot of know-how about cartoons. One of his cartoons has been used for figure 63. Just

"HELLO, IS THAT THE FIRE BRIGADE?"

Fig. 64

a few wavy lines depict mountains, and squiggly ones have been used for small stones. A few strokes are all that were needed to shade trousers. John uses a dip pen with a bottle of black drawing ink. See how a variation in line is obtained by this type of nib. He likes occasionally to take off to the hills, so he used his interest to spark off the excellent idea for this cartoon. Mint cake is eaten by mountain walkers as a fast way to obtain energy. I admire John's clean, open style of sketching.

Figure 64, also by John, reflects his wide interest in art. Note how little detail has been used yet all the necessary information is there. Man's stupidity and accidents are two very common themes used by humorists.

Assignments
1. Re-draw figures 63 and 64 but create your own people to express the same ideas.
2. Study three published cartoons; then think out variations or twists on the ideas used. Draw your adaptations.
3. Look at figure 65. Then invent what Super Doodle could do next. Draw your idea as a cartoon.

Fig. 65

10

DRAW YOUR OWN
GREETINGS CARDS

Designing greetings cards in order to sell them to commercial concerns is a tough, highly competitive business. Many greetings card companies have their own artists and those that do not tend to pay poor rates. You can, however, easily produce your own cartoon cards to cover any event. Your family or friends will, I assure you, be pleased to receive one of your little gems on a special occasion. There are numerous days honoured by greetings cards: Mothers', Fathers' and Grandparents' days; Christmas, New Year and Easter; Valentine, birthday, wedding, birth, retirement, promotion and congratulations — just to mention a few. There are many outlets for your cartoon talents.

Materials to use

You can draw your designs on thick drawing paper, artist's board, or good cardboard. Use your normal drawing pen for the sketches. Your finished work can be enhanced by the use of a spot of colour. Use coloured pencils, highlighters, water colours or poster paints.

Look through old cards to decide what size you will use. Open one out then measure it. Notice which side the cover design is on and which page has the caption, if any. Cut out a similar size blank card and fold it in half. (A ruler is handy for this. With it you can first score a folding line down the middle of your paper using a sharp point such as a steel knitting needle or an awl.) Remember to keep the front cover with the fold on your left before you begin, lightly, to pencil in a design. Ink it in when you are satisfied.

HAPPY CHRISTMAS

Fig. 66 Snowmen are easy to draw.

An easy start for you

The Christmas season heralds the exchange of millions of greetings cards. There are many possible subjects to cartoon but a particularly easy one is snowmen. This is little more than a controlled doodle. You could draw a cartoon snowman with one of your eyes closed. Look at figure 66. This idea came to me out of the proverbial blue. I quickly jotted it down. The caption could just as appropriately have been placed inside the

Fig. 67   Aim for simple drawing.

card. This design is ideal for a tall, slim Christmas card. The finished drawing could be improved by the use of colour. A little blue added to indicate shadow, a grey winter sky, a few red-nosed snowmen and that is about it. There is another snowman, with offspring, for you to look at in figure 67. Also included is a cartoon robin which is a very popular bird for Christmas cards. Copy figures 66 and 67 for practice.

Visual jokes, the sort that do not require a caption, are very popular world-wide because no language translations are needed. Figure 68 is my example of this type of gag. See how everything has been drawn with as few lines as possible. A seasonal greeting could easily be put inside. Re-draw this one with your own characters.

Fig. 68   A visual cartoon.

Fig. 69 Animal cartoons are popular.

Cartoon animals

You may have noticed that scores of greetings card designers use animals to put over a message. Horses, dogs, cats, mice, reindeer and many other species regularly crop up. Figure 69 was drawn to show you how one idea can be used at least twice. You can often do this. Ideas beget ideas; the more that you think of, the more that flit into your mind. Take note of how I have used a few short pen strokes to suggest fur in the cat. Draw your versions of these ideas.

Fig. 70   Are you late with birthday cards?

I sometimes forget a friend's birthday but try to make up for my weakness by sending an original cartoon to bridge the gap. Figure 70 is a copy of one that I sent to a chum several weeks after the event. On the original card I put the lower caption on the inside. This cartoon elephant is another simple sketch. Try drawing your idea of a gentle giant.

I have used the giraffe frequently in cartoons. It has a funny natural shape so it is easy to turn into a comic drawing. Figure 71 was drawn for a friend's wedding. See how I drew

CONGRATULATIONS

Fig. 71 Animal cartoons are easy to think out.

the female giraffe slightly smaller than the male. I also added in eyelashes. A similar idea could be used for congratulating a birth. This would simply require drawing in a baby giraffe. Why not try it yourself?

People inspire cartoon ideas

I have previously mentioned how people can inspire cartoon ideas. It might be something they say, do, or wear. An example of this happened on my cartoon course when one student bought a new hat for herself. The headgear gave me the idea of a witch. The lady concerned, bless her, was far removed from being a witch. She was, in fact, very witty, generous and talented. The original thought evolved into a funny scene of the sort I draw just to amuse my friends. Thus figure 72 is the

Fig. 72   A cartoon based on a real person.

result of a nice lady buying a straw hat! Isn't it strange how the
mind works? This cartoon also shows how you can add words
to make a joke or put over information. Now draw your
cartoon witch.

Assignments
1. Design a birthday card.
2. Invent a funny cartoon for a Valentine card.
3. Produce a Christmas card for your favourite person.

Fig. 73

11

CARTOON YOUR DAY

There are more ways than one for you to illustrate a day in your life. You could feature yourself as the central character around which all the action, whether true or imagined, happens, or you could draw all the events as if looking through a video camera. The latter method would not require you to depict yourself as a funny cartoon, but, in my opinion, might not be as amusing as portraying yourself. Imagine, for example, that you have been awakened by your pet dog leaping onto your bed and licking your face. You could draw this incident showing exactly that, but if you record your life through your eyes, you could only draw a close-up of a dog's face.

You are so comical

I am sure that you have the humour and skill to turn yourself into a funny sketch. You need not make yourself life-like. You already know what you look like but when you come to draw yourself as a cartoon character do not be tempted to use a mirror because this reflects the opposite image to the one seen by other people. If, for example, your hair is parted on the left

Fig. 74   How I turned myself into a cartoon figure.

side and you draw what you view, the sketch will show the parting on your right side. You can, however, use photographs. You should aim to produce a cartoon figure that is amusing to look at. This means that any tiny trace of vanity which you may have must be banished!

I do not expect you to draw anything which I am not prepared to draw so I have forced myself to transform the

Fig. 75   How to change real people into cartoons.

cartoon figure drawn by Pat for figure 62 in chapter 9. Study figure 74 to see how I have exaggerated my delicate features. Note how my slim, power-packed body has been altered. My tiny feet — admittedly not seen in Pat's cartoon — have been swopped for two whoppers. There are some who may think that I have improved on the original version. Carefully study this drawing. I can't bear to look at it!

You may be a young lady who has the looks of a top model, film star, or a Miss World. The sort of woman who can instantly stop traffic, obtain immediate attention from railway

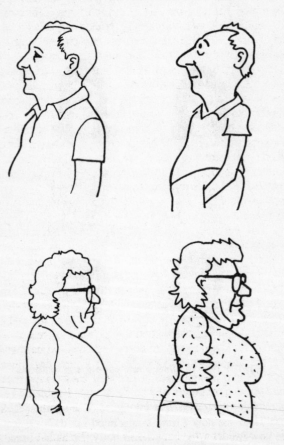

Fig. 76 Change ordinary people into extraordinary cartoons.

porters, and twist any man round a long, beautifully painted
fingernail. Perhaps you are a young man with such sickening
good looks that the opposite sex swoon or shriek when you
swagger into view. The sort of chap other men want to thump
on sight, girls fight over, and wealthy, elderly ladies leave vast
inheritances to. On the other hand you might consider that you
are Mr, Mrs, or Miss Average with such an ordinary
appearance that your pet dog or cat, postman, milkman, boss
and members of your own family quickly forget who you are.
Don't worry — I will show you how to change your normal
appearance into a funny cartoon character!

Look carefully at figure 75. See how the good-looking are
transformed quite painlessly: the cartoon characters still have
some resemblance to the real person. Figure 76 shows how
ordinary folk can be made into extraordinary comical
characters quite easily. Could you be as wicked with yourself?
Of course you can! Get busy with a pencil. Invent a cartoon of
you. Try out your results on friends or family. Look for a
glimmer of gold, a smile; listen for a bit of magic, a chuckle.
These are the signs that you have won.

Dawn draw
Now that you have become a cartoon character you can start
to depict a comical day in your life. Most of us begin our day
by waking up. Think hard about the way you come out of the
land of dreams. Do you have an abrupt awakening caused by
noisy children, your spouse, pets, a massed chorus of birds, or
the persistent ringing of an alarm clock? Do you slowly come
to life? If so, what do you feel like? Is it as if the end of the
world is nigh, or wishing that you hadn't lived it up the
previous evening? There are dozens of potential cartoon ideas
from the single happening of starting a new day. Figure 77
illustrates two possibilities. Notice how background detail has
been kept to a minimum and how a thought bubble and a word
balloon have been used to tell the story. Use similar techniques
yourself.

Next consider what happens to you at breakfast time. Is the
meal hurriedly gobbled down because you have to catch a train

or a bus, or drive to work? Are you retired? Can you spend until lunch-time on breakfast? Do you eat alone or share the table with a huge family? What sort of things can and do go wrong? Were the porridge, bacon and toast all right, or did one or more of them get burnt to a cinder? Did you find your partner or spouse, and/or the children all in good humour, or

Fig. 77   Draw ways you could wake up.

was one of them feeling rather frail? Are there ever disputes over possession or content of the daily newspaper, the size of the kippers, the freshness of the cornflakes or the coffee, or the state of the weather? Remember that impending disaster, minor

Fig. 78 Ideas from two popular sports.

accidents, or funny remarks can give birth to many cartoon ideas. Never lose sight of the fact that YOU are the star comic of your tale.

Mid-morning madness

You might have picked one day of a weekend or one of your normal working days to immortalise. Perhaps you could try to work on both. The next episode to fill is that between breakfast and lunch. How do you usually spend this time? Maybe it is a Saturday when you normally rush off to a golf course to play a round with friends. What could go wrong here? A wheel could come off your golf trolley; you may score a hole in one and then have to buy a round of drinks for everybody in sight; you could consecutively whack three golf balls into a lake hazard, or lose one down a rabbit hole (this once happened to me). Sport has many hidden minor dangers, irritations, accidents and triumphs. I feel sure that you could easily hatch a few ideas that are connected to your favourite sport or hobby. I have featured two popular sports in figure 78. In the golf joke see how sand has been suggested by lots of dots. Lashing rain, in the fishing gag, was drawn with broken lines.

Maybe you are a housewife who has sixteen hungry children, an idle husband, a tumble-down home and elderly parents to look after? If you are in this unfortunate position I am mighty flattered that you are reading this book! Seriously though, whatever your situation is, there are hundreds of funny cartoon ideas that could arise from quite normal activities. Think about possible human errors and weaknesses and then apply a few of them to your great cartoon story.

You may well be one of the millions of people who have to go to work. I have had many different jobs in my eventful life. They range from test-riding motor bikes, to office work, administration in a busy hospital, health promotion projects and various teaching posts. All these occupations sparked off cartoon ideas. Look at figure 79. This idea of mine was published in a national newspaper over twenty years ago, but I have re-used it by bringing it up-to-date with a word processor.

Just before starting to write this chapter, for example, I went along to teach my regular weekly class of retired people how to draw. One of my students has a sparkling but sometimes outrageous sense of humour. She came out with a remark which amused us all. I immediately drew a cartoon of her, but changed her words into thoughts. We all enjoyed a good laugh

Fig. 79   "Fire the person under that lot!"

at the result which you can see in figure 80. I drew this with an ordinary fountain pen that had been filled with black drawing ink. Notice the variable width of the lines. People often come up with a funny comment that provides a ready-made cartoon caption or idea. Mentally go through your employment, the staff, conditions, environment and everything connected to your work. You will soon be able to pick out comical events to use in your side-splitting yarn.

Afternoon hiccups

How are your afternoons filled? Are you grafting away, playing polo, gardening, visiting friends, baking a cake, hang gliding, decorating or, maybe, learning to drive? Who are you

Fig. 80   A funny remark cartooned.

likely to meet? Would they be family, chums, or strangers? Would some of them perhaps be people to whom you are forced to be polite despite their not being deserving of your outstanding charm and good manners? Do you tend to live in an ivory tower from where you occasionally descend to cast a few priceless pearls to the swine, or are you one of the swine? Use your humour on your afternoon happenings.

And so to bed

Are some of your evenings spent recovering from a hard shift down a mine, a sumptuous seven course lunch, a tough game of football, a tedious "Superware" party, or what? Do you pass the hours watching television, courting, meeting pals, furthering your education or feathering your nest? There are endless possibilities here to work on.

Now turn your attention to what happens when you go to bed. The mind boggles at the fund of possible ideas that might come from this simple action. Burglars could be on the prowl, as could be ghosts, vampire bats, witches, mothers-in-law, children, pets and other things. Accidents such as fire, flood and natural disasters might occur.

I hope that some of the ideas expressed in this chapter will trigger off your mind to produce brilliantly funny drawings for your epic story.

Assignments

1. Write in detail your normal day from dawn to dusk. Then think out an exaggerated version of what you have put down.
2. Plan ten cartoons to illustrate your funny normal day.
3. Draw out these cartoons in ink.

Fig. 81

12

RECORD YOUR LIFE IN CARTOONS

By working through all the chapters of this book you will have drawn scores of cartoons and learned enough tricks of the trade to be able now to tackle creating the story of your unique life with cartoons. Many of us enjoy keeping a diary of, or talking about our lives; you may find this project even more interesting and amusing. But it would be a daunting task to try to do this solely by funny drawings because you would need to produce many hundreds of them. It is necessary to add a commentary, either as hand written or typed text, written *in with* the pictures. I much prefer this latter method. I use a cheap fountain pen filled with black drawing ink and good quality typing paper. You may not have much experience of writing so I will give you a useful tip. Write your story as if you were telling it to a friend. This is called a conversational style of writing. It is one I have always used in my books, stories and articles. You are about to become a writer as well as a talented cartoonist!

Getting a likeness

The artist who can draw representations of people by exaggeration has reached the pinnacle of his profession, and earned the title of caricaturist. Examples of this specialist skill are to be seen in political cartoons used by newspapers the world over. The raw material of caricaturists is, of course, the famous and infamous celebrities who happen to be in the news at the time. How do those talented cartoonists succeed, day after day, in churning out top-class work? They do it by hard graft, keen observation and expert drawing.

If, for example, you want to produce a humorous sketch of your favourite Uncle Bill (the wealthy one) you will have to study carefully his face, build and characteristics. You then have to decide which parts of uncle have to be exaggerated so that anyone who knows him would recognize, from your cartoon, who it was. Uncle Bill might be an ex-boxer complete with broken nose, cauliflower ears and a battered, lop-sided face. If so, characterization of him will be easy. I have drawn my version of such an uncle in figure 82. Take a look at this before copying it.

The chances are, however, that he is a nice, ordinary-looking gentleman with hardly any outstanding features. This makes the job harder but not impossible. If Uncle Bill has thinning hair, a beaming smile, laughter lines round his eyes and is sturdily built, for instance, you have something to start on. All the features mentioned could be *slightly exaggerated* to produce a funny drawing, and ensure a slice of his vast fortune for yourself! Go back for another look at figures 75 and 76 to

Fig. 82   Some faces are easy to caricature.

see what I mean.

Often we need see but little in order to recognize someone we know, be they a relative, friend or foe. I once drew a caricature of a walking leader from *one item* of clothing which he wore. He loped along at speed so I was always behind him, but I noticed that he always had a woolly hat pulled right down over his right ear. It was his hallmark. I drew the cartoon you can see in figure 83. Any of his friends who saw my sketch knew instantly who it was. You can use small, known eccentricities of your intended victims. He or she might have a different way of standing, walking or gesturing; the person concerned may wear outlandish clothes or have some other little give away which can be used.

After hours of practice I can now draw a cartoon of almost anyone. Some people, however, are very difficult to caricature quickly. These are the plain, undistinguished folk; the kind who never stand out in a crowd. When my subject is a tough one I spend as long as possible scrutinizing the face and body. Then I use a pencil to produce up to a dozen rough sketches of the person. Once I can get the mouth-line, eyebrows, nose

Fig. 83 An item of clothing can be a give away to identity.

Fig. 84   Distinctive clothes are helpful.

and hair style right I know that the cartoon will eventually appear. You might try this method yourself.

Children do not have strong features, age lines or wrinkles, so they are hard to caricature, but what they wear can be of help. Today, with so much choice about, children tend to wear what they like, and this is often quite different gear from that which their chums have. You can use their fashion fad to help establish their identity. I have drawn examples for figure 84 to show you how to set about this task. When sketching children remember to exaggerate the size of the head, but keep noses small and avoid fussy lines.

If you find that you have a talent or at least a keen interest in caricaturing, consider reading my *Paperfront* book, 'The Right Way To Draw People'. It deals in depth with the skill of sketching people. The special techniques involved are well worthwhile developing. You are in demand if you can turn your friends and other people into funny cartoons.

The happiest days of your life?

You may vividly recall incidents in your babyhood, or maybe your earliest recollections, like those of most people, are of when you first began to talk, walk or go to school. Do you still remember the first school that you went to? Was it a modern building or something out of Charles Dickens's era? What were your teachers like?

When you moved on to a higher school what was that like? How did life change for you? Who became your mates? Were the teachers better than before or worse?

When I was at grammar school we had art classes with which I did not much bother because I considered the teacher to be hopeless. I never saw him draw or paint; possibly he could not. When he was called up for military service we were delighted to be allowed to romp over to the girls' grammar school to share their excellent art mistress. Before the days of co-education many boys, including me, were terribly shy of girls. Consequently, when we joined forces for art, our shyness caused us to work hard while the girls teased us. The boys passed their art examinations but the girls did not ...

Some of our teachers were very good, others were bad, a few were indifferent. We tended to punish or play-up the weak ones. We once lowered a teacher's desk and chair through a class room window down onto a path outside the building. Then when he arrived to teach us we pleaded ignorance as to where the missing furniture was. On another occasion we locked out a teacher then acted as though we could not open the door. We gave the poor man a hard time. I do not remember if we were caned for these small acts of rebellion but I expect some of us were. I hope that reading about my school days will prompt you to write a page or two about yours.

Fig. 85   What activities did you have?

Teenage years

Concentrate on your teenage years. What did you do? Did you take part in sports? Were you at ease with the opposite sex? Did you go to parties, musical events, or travel abroad? What

Fig. 86 What did you do?

good causes did you support? There are a million things which you may have done. Jot down some of them. Make them a mixture of good and bad. Now plan them as funny cartoons.

You, as a young adult

Can you remember celebrating your 18th or 21st birthday? What did you do? What was your occupation at the time? Were you courting, married, or divorced twice? Was there the patter of little footsteps in your life? Did the thud of the bailiff's boots interrupt your progress? Figure 85 shows two possible teenage activities. See how the horse and the car have been drawn simply. Copy these.

The armed forces turned me loose when I was 22 years old. Was I glad! Being interested in sport, I played parks' league cricket. I also played table tennis, and rode a powerful motor bike in trials and scrambles. I took on the job of helping at a youth club, overcame my shyness of the opposite sex, and learned how to write saleable short stories through a good correspondence course. In general I had a very happy time. How was it for you? Notice, in figure 86, how bikes and boats can be drawn.

Your thirties

In our thirties, most of us have settled down, started a family, undertaken a huge mortgage, decided on a career and perhaps become a little wiser than we were. Cast your mind back to those years. Were you married then? Were your pastimes or hobbies like those illustrated in figure 87?

With whom did you live? What did you love or hate? How did you get along with other people? There are countless incidents from this period which you can turn into funny drawings such as the ones used for figure 88. If you are in your thirties right now you could keep a cartoon diary of your life. The record would contain your funny observations on the world in general and be a contemporary account of modern life. You could have a best seller!

Fig. 87   What pastimes did you have?

Middle age

Years ago 'middle age' was accepted as applying to anyone who was over 40 years old. Today the same term covers all of us who are between 40 and 60. This is because we now have

Fig. 88 Were your thirties eventful?

a longer life expectancy. Three cheers for that!

Middle age can be pleasant, boring or traumatic, depending

on what happens to the person concerned. It has been said that life begins at 40. I don't know who put about this rubbish. It is quite untrue. Life can begin whenever you want it to. In my own case it all happened rather later in life — after I had discovered the power of positive thinking.

Fig. 89   Retirement should be a happy time.

If you are middle aged, have you rebelled against your life, wife, spouse, children, job, Council, Government, or are you sedate, untroubled, and calm? Most folk have a lot of upheaval and many stressful times during their middle years. All events can be turned into cartoons: tragedy can soon become comedy. Make a note of the various happenings in your middle life.

Senior citizen

More and more people join the ranks of the retired class. Retirement offers a great chance to start a completely new life but, sadly, for many it also means financial hardship. We are, however, much luckier than were our forefathers. We are free, more or less, to do what we want, go where we want to, learn new skills and make each day a holiday. For what more could we wish?

If you are retired what do you do? Do you gallop up to your local post office to collect your hard-earned pension each week, or do you send your chauffeur in the second Rolls Royce? Do you meet other senior citizens? Do you keep fit by doing household chores, shopping, or going on rambles, climbing mountains, hang gliding, or what? There should be plenty of cartoons in and around your life at this time. If you have yet to reach this level of your life remember that you can still include elderly folk in your life story. They are usually easy to draw. Some look like living cartoons! Look carefully at figure 89. Note my use of shading. Copy these and then apply the principles either to yourself or to people you know.

Now you have come to the end of this book I hope that you are eager to start the record of your life by first writing a script and then illustrating it with your funny drawings. Begin by having a good think and jotting down notes. Then stir your pencil into action. Good luck. Have fun!

Fig. 90

By the same author

THE RIGHT WAY TO DRAW

Anyone can learn to draw. But doing so with confidence only comes quickly if you get the basics right. Here Mark Linley explains the principles to you, step-by-step, just as if he were teaching you personally during one of his many art classes.

Discover how to *look* properly. Learn from your inevitable early 'disasters' and get things in the right perspective. You'll soon see how easy it is to draw people, animals, trees, buildings, views and still life.

THE RIGHT WAY TO DRAW PEOPLE

Mark Linley shows how drawing people can be fun! Within moments of opening this book, you will be drawing people, and amazing yourself and friends with your success.

THE RIGHT WAY TO DRAW LANDSCAPES

Mark Linley's infectious enthusiasm spills into your pen as you interpret his work and develop your own style. Suddenly you discover at your finger-tips the ability to portray those fine trees, rocks, mountains, water, etc. that 'make' a picture.

Uniform with this book

WINE MAKING THE NATURAL WAY

Recipes using step-by-step "no frills" natural methods of wine making have been gathered in this book to enable you to produce a splendid array of country-style wines for an outlay of only pence per bottle. Ingredients are used as close to their original form as possible to safeguard healing properties (often long established), retain valuable oils and scents while extracting maximum flavour, vitamins and goodness.

EASYMADE WINE & COUNTRY DRINKS

The traditional recipes collected here have been carefully adapted to make best use of current widely available and inexpensive aids whilst retaining their original economy and simplicity. A clever wine calendar tells you when to make each wine throughout the year to make best use of cheap seasonal crops. A standard basic recipe is included in case you want to try out an unusual wine of your own for which no detailed recipe is given.

HOME WINEMAKING THE RIGHT WAY

As well as the major elements of home winemaking this book includes a detailed analysis of how and why various types of wine differ and shows how to train your palate to judge their relative qualities. This is the key to mastery both of what to do when in trouble, and of the subtle adjustments which can transform a moderate wine into an award-winner.

In the same series

WRITE YOUR OWN WILL

Everyone over 18 should make a Will, even though most of us may feel that we do not have a great deal to dispose of. If it is simply a question of leaving a modest amount of property or money to the immediate family or to charity, then this book contains all you need to make a proper legal Will yourself. A special feature of the book is the chapter of *sample Wills* designed to cover most circumstances.

The Right Way To WRITE YOUR OWN C.V.

Anybody who has been made redundant or who wants to change jobs, needs a proper C.V. (*Curriculum Vitae*) — and it needs to be good enough to *stand out* among dozens or perhaps hundreds of others. John Clarke is one of Britain's foremost professional C.V. compilers. He has written hundreds of C.V.s for people seeking every imaginable kind of employment. In this book he explains the strategy he has developed which really *works* — his C.V.s enjoy a rate of success many times greater than average.

Uniform with this book

In our Right Way series
(Large format paperback size)

PROBATE The Right Way To Prove A Will

This book explains how to apply for Probate on someone's death (or Letters of Administration if there is no Will) and how to administer the Estate. Clearly and concisely it steers the reader around the few pitfalls that do exist, lays down the sequence of things to do, and gives some basic advice on more technical matters.

YOUR VOICE

A simple but valuable guide for those who want to polish and improve their most potent means of communication: the voice. For some reason, while we spend a lot of time and money trying to make ourselves *look* good we neglect how we *sound*. This book helps redress the balance. The idea is not to get rid of regional accents or create a neutral voice but, through the use of crisp consonants and well shaped vowels, to bring out clear, dynamic and persuasive speech.

HOW TO RUN A QUIZ

This book is for the growing number of people who run quizzes. Discover how to set up a "Social Quiz" for teams of equal size and see how to arrange "gamble" and "table" questions. Try new styles for the "Pub Quiz" or "Team Quiz". Experiment with the fast and furious "Frantic Quiz", or focus on the "Spotlight Quiz". A good quiz uses up an alarming quantity of questions, so the book also contains over 2,000 carefully researched questions and answers.

OUR PUBLISHING POLICY

HOW WE CHOOSE

Our policy is to consider every deserving manuscript and we can give special editorial help where an author is an authority on his subject but an inexperienced writer. We are rigorously selective in the choice of books we publish. We set the highest standards of editorial quality and accuracy. This means that a *Paperfront* is easy to understand and delightful to read. Where illustrations are necessary to convey points of detail, these are drawn up by a subject specialist artist from our panel.

HOW WE KEEP PRICES LOW

We aim for the big seller. This enables us to order enormous print runs and achieve the lowest price for you. Unfortunately, this means that you will not find in the *Paperfront* list any titles on obscure subjects of minority interest only. These could not be printed in large enough quantities to be sold for the low price at which we offer this series.

We sell almost all our *Paperfronts* at the same unit price. This saves a lot of fiddling about in our clerical departments and helps us to give you world-beating value. Under this system, the longer titles are offered at a price which we believe to be unmatched by any publisher in the world.

OUR DISTRIBUTION SYSTEM

Because of the competitive price, and the rapid turnover, *Paperfronts* are possibly the most profitable line a bookseller can handle. They are stocked by the best bookshops all over the world. It may be that your bookseller has run out of stock of a particular title. If so, he can order more from us at any time—we have a fine reputation for "same day" despatch, and we supply any order, however small (even a single copy), to any bookseller who has an account with us. We prefer you to buy from your bookseller, as this reminds him of the strong underlying public demand for *Paperfronts*. Members of the public who live in remote places, or who are housebound, or whose local bookseller is unco-operative, can order direct from us by post.

FREE

If you would like an up-to-date list of all *Paperfront* titles currently available, send a stamped self-addressed envelope to
ELLIOT RIGHT WAY BOOKS, BRIGHTON RD.,
LOWER KINGSWOOD, TADWORTH, SURREY, KT20 6TD, UK.